Illustrated by Mark Busacca, Edwin Esquivel, Emi Fukawa, Doug Scott, Vadim Vahrameev, Hanako Wakiyama and Bill Yenne.

Printed in Italy

Series UPC: 39440

Bible Classics

Joseph and the Coat of Many Colors

Modern Publishing
A Division of Unisystems, Inc.
New York, New York 10022
Series UPC: 39440

A long time ago in a land called Hebron, there lived a good man named Jacob. He had 12 sons.

Of all his sons, Jacob loved Joseph best. Jacob made Joseph a beautiful coat that seemed to have every color of the rainbow in it. That coat became known as Joseph's "coat of many colors." Jacob's other sons were angry and jealous of their father's love for Joseph.

Joseph had two amazing dreams. He decided to tell his father and his brothers about them. In one dream, his brothers' sheaves of grain were bowing down to Joseph's sheaf.

The other dream was about the sun, the moon and eleven stars bowing down to Joseph. His brothers thought that Joseph was lying and bragging about the dreams, and their hatred of him increased.

A short time later, the brothers decided to kill Joseph. The oldest brother, Reuben, talked them out of their plan to kill him. Instead, they took Joseph's coat and threw him into an empty well.

Reuben planned to come back later that night and rescue Joseph from the well. Before he could do so, the other brothers sold Joseph to some slave traders for 20 pieces of silver.

When Reuben found out what his brothers had done, he was very upset. The other brothers tore Joseph's coat and dipped it in goat's blood.

They showed their father the coat. Jacob was sure that a wild animal had eaten Joseph. No one could comfort him in his distress over the loss of Joseph.

The traders took Joseph to Egypt, where they sold him to Potipher, the captain of Pharoah's guard. Later, because Joseph was such a good man, Potipher made him the chief servant of his whole house.

Potipher's wife wanted Joseph to betray her husband, but Joseph was loyal to Potipher. When he would not obey Potipher's wife, she became very angry.

Potipher's wife was vengeful and made up a lie about Joseph. She had him thrown into jail, but even there, God took care of Joseph.

The keeper of the jail put Joseph in charge of all of the other prisoners.

Some years later, while Joseph was still in jail, Pharaoh had two strange dreams. None of his best advisers knew what the dreams meant, but a man who had been in prison remembered that Joseph had been able to decipher dreams.

Pharaoh sent for Joseph.

Joseph said that the dream meant that Egypt would have seven years of good crops and seven years of famine. Egypt should store up food to use later. Pharaoh was amazed at Joseph's wisdom.

He made Joseph second in command over all of Egypt and gave Joseph fine clothes to wear. He put a gold chain around Joseph's neck and put his own ring on Joseph's finger.

Joseph married an Egyptian girl and they had two sons. The crops increased year after year for seven years, just as he had predicted.

Then the seven bad years came. The people were hungry. Pharaoh told them to go to Joseph to find out what they should do.

Joseph was now the governor of the land. He sold food to all who came. His father, Jacob, sent his sons to buy food from Egypt. Joseph knew who they were, but his brothers didn't recognize Joseph. It had been 20 years since they last saw him.

Joseph decided to test his brothers to see if they had changed. They proved that they had become much better men but still, Joseph did not tell them that he was their brother.

Soon, the brothers came back for more food. This time Joseph told them who he was. He also told them that it was God's will that he was brought to live in Egypt. Pharaoh heard the whole story and was happy for Joseph.

Pharaoh arranged with Joseph to have his family move to Egypt. They would share in the riches of Pharaoh's kingdom.

Joseph's family was glad to go to Egypt. Joseph's father, Jacob, was overjoyed to find his son alive.

Jacob lived for many more years. He gave his blessing to Joseph's sons. He knew they would be good men, just like their father, Joseph.